LET'S BUILD A CAR

Written by Margaret A. Schaefer

Illustrated by Patrick T. McRae

IDEALS CHILDREN'S BOOKS
Nashville, Tennessee

ACKNOWLEDGMENTS

Ideals Publishing Corporation would like to thank Chrysler Motors,
General Motors, and the Motor Vehicle Manufacturers Association
of the United States for their aid in preparing this book.

Published by Ideals Publishing Corporation
Nelson Place at Elm Hill Pike
Nashville, Tennessee 37214

Printed and bound in the United States of America.

Library of Congress Cataloging-in-Publication Data

Schaefer, Margaret A., 1963–
      Let's build a car / by Margaret A. Schaefer ; illustrated by
Patrick T. McRae.
          p.   cm.
      Summary: Explains and identifies the steps used in putting
together a typical car from constructing the frame to painting to
final roll-off.
      ISBN 0-8249-8431-5
      1. Automobiles--Design and construction--Juvenile literature.
[1. Automobiles--Design and construction.]   I. McRae, Patrick, ill.
II. Title.
   TL147.S38   1990
629.23--dc20   89-29426
                                                  CIP
                                                  AC

To my son, Ryan, for his love of cars

—Patrick McRae

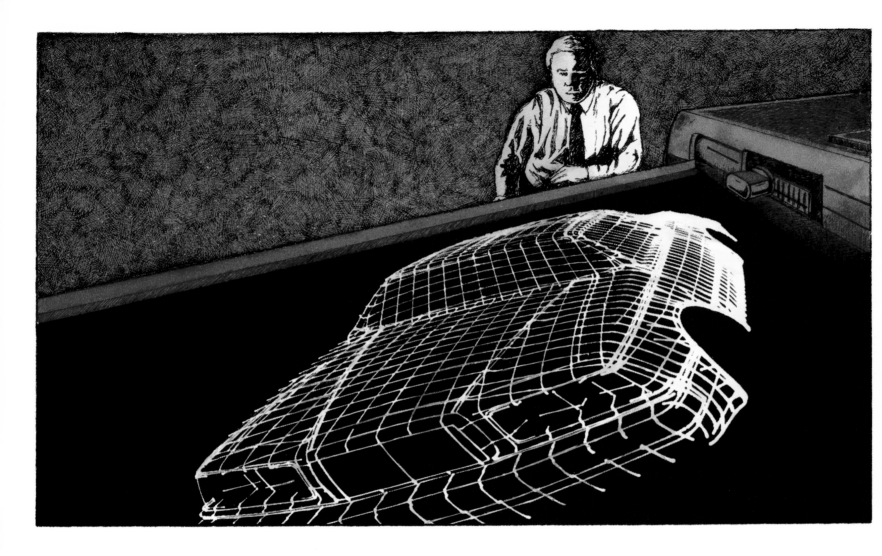

A car begins in the mind of a designer. Using a process called *CAD*, or *computer-aided design*, the designer actually draws the car on a computer screen. Line by line he draws the frame, the body, and each part of the car.

The designer then turns the car around on the screen. He can look at it from the top, the bottom, or either side of the car. He may reshape a panel or move a piece from one place to another until the car appears just as he wants it to.

Workers then build models following the design of the car. The first models may be small, like toy cars. They can be made of clay or plastic or even wood.

The last model will be as big as a finished car. Workers shape and mold clay until the model is exactly like the design, inside and out. Not only do they create the body of the car, but they also mold the inside, including the dashboard, gear shift, and arm rests.

Using the model and computer design as guides, designers and engineers build a *prototype*. A prototype is a car built by hand. It works as the finished car will in every detail, but it is very slow and expensive to build. It is built for testing.

Engineers test this prototype in many ways, such as placing it in a giant *wind tunnel* with winds of up to 150 miles per hour to see how the wind moves around the car. If the wind moves in certain patterns, the car will move through the air more easily and need less gas to run.

Test drivers take the prototype over rough roads to test the steering and tires. They drive it for long distances without stopping to make sure it is durable and comfortable.

The prototype also undergoes a crash test, using dummies in place of people. After the crash, engineers determine how safe the car is by measuring the damage to the dummies and the car.

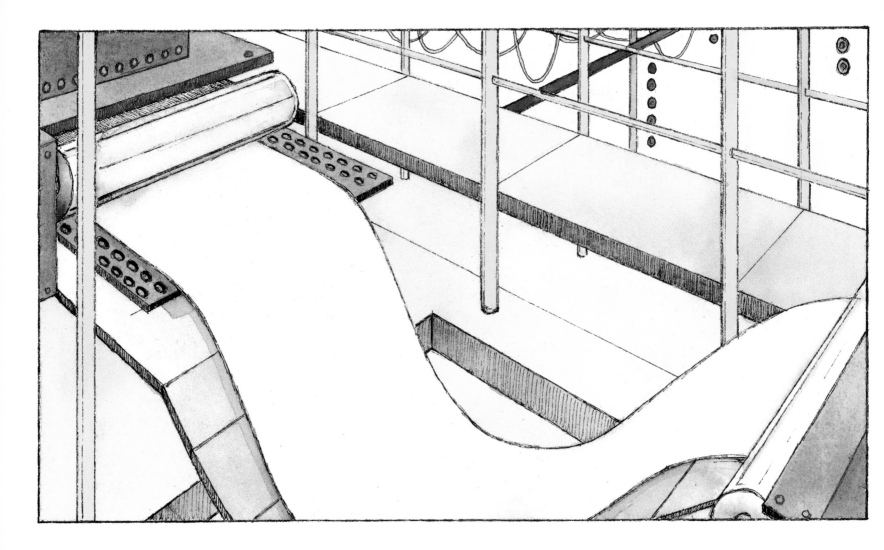

Our prototype has passed its tests. It is now ready for *mass production*. Before mass production can begin, however, the engine, windshield, wheels, and many other parts are made in smaller factories throughout the country. The manufacturers ship these parts to the huge *assembly plant* to be used in constructing the car.

The car's body begins at the blanking and stamping plant. Here a huge roll of thin steel is fed into a *blanking press*.

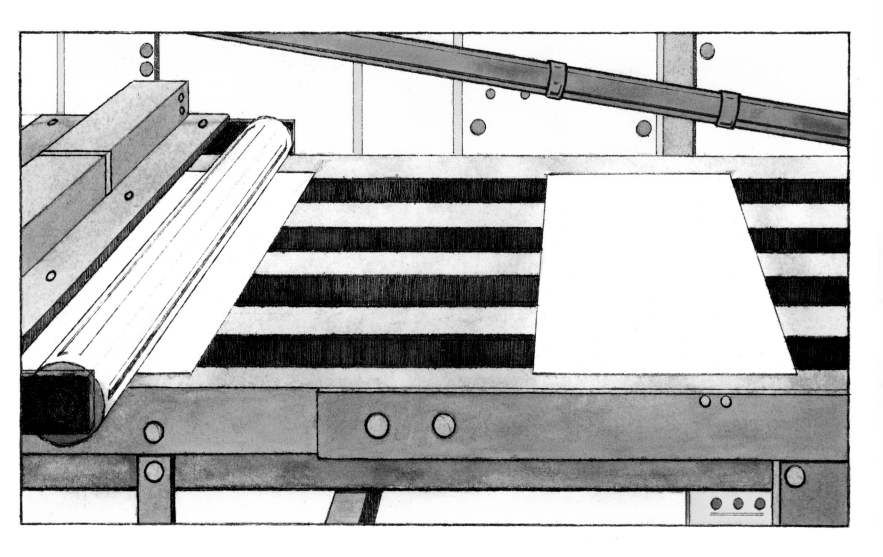

The blanking press is as tall as a two-story house. It shakes and booms as it cuts out pieces of metal like a giant cookie cutter. These pieces, called panels, are cut to the approximate sizes of the car parts they will become.

As these panels come out of the blanking press, they are stacked until being moved to the *stamping machines*. The stamping machine molds the metal into the various parts of the car's body.

As the panel of steel moves through the stamping machine, holes are drilled, sections are cut, and corners are raised. These pieces come out of the stamping machine as doors, trunks, and hoods. They are stacked and ready to be shipped to the assembly plant.

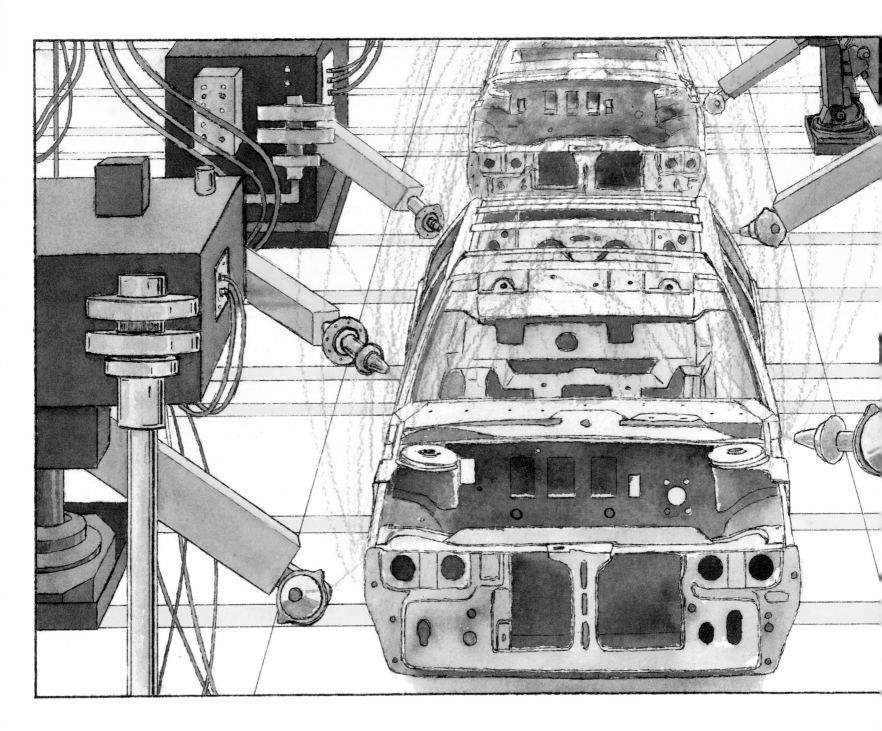

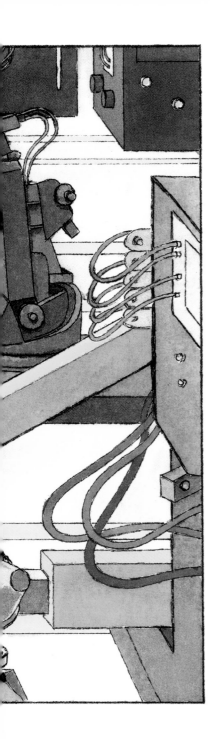

Now our car is ready to be assembled. We begin in the *body shop* of the assembly plant. The *underbody* and *side frames* are loosely joined together and the roof is placed on top. Robots weld, or join together, the pieces by heating the two spots of metal until they *fuse*. There may be as many 5,000 welding spots on one car, and robots can accomplish this task more quickly than humans.

With the top, bottom, and sides of the car securely joined, workers must attach the doors, trunk, and hood. They move the pieces into position and then bolt them into place. The body of our car is now complete and ready to move to the paint shop.

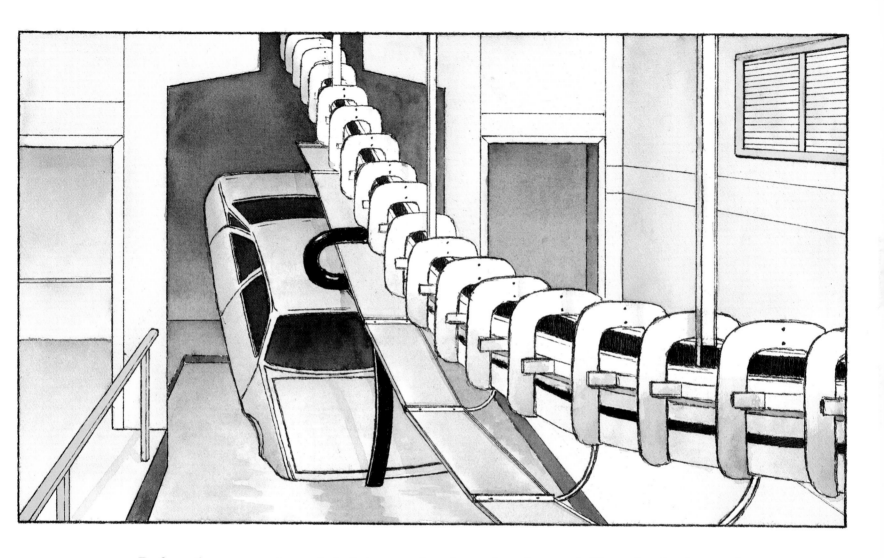

Before the car can be painted, it must be cleaned and coated. Huge hooks lower the car body into a cleaning solution and shake it about like the clothes in a washing machine. The car is lifted and dipped again, this time into an *anti-corrosion bath*. This process protects the car's metal from rust.

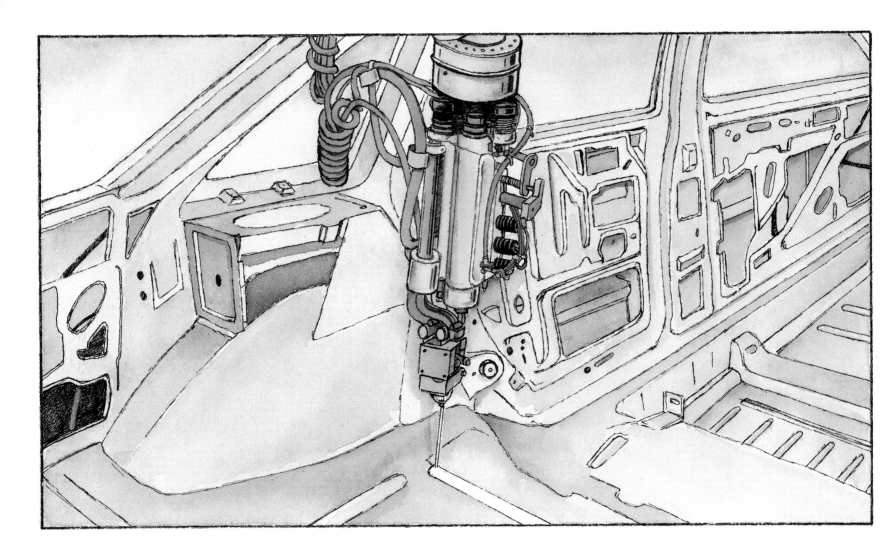

Two steps remain before the car can be painted. The metal must first be sprayed with a coat of *gray primer*. Paint will stick better to this than to the bare metal of the body.

After the primer, mechanical guns apply *sealant* to the seams of the car body. This closes up any gaps between the metal parts and keeps water from leaking into the body.

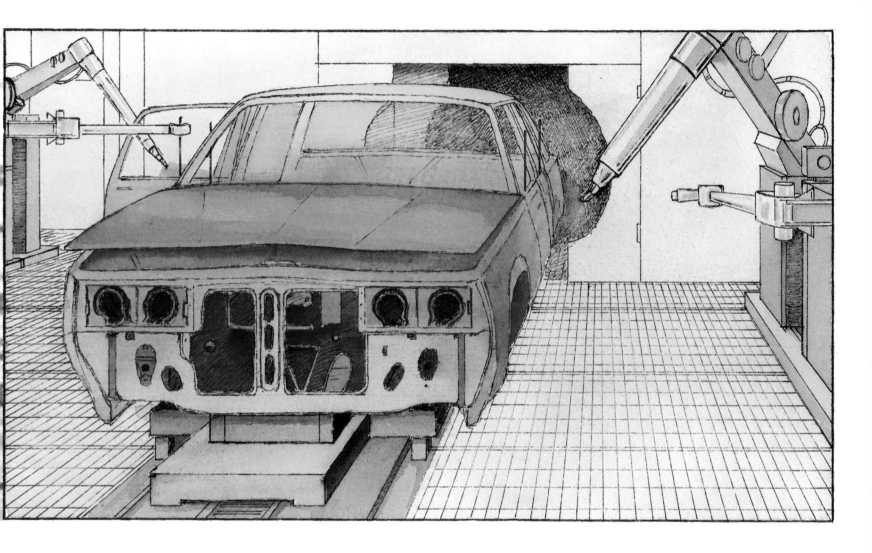

Our car is now ready for the *paint booth*. This area must be kept extremely clean because dirt and dust cause bumps under the paint.

Robotic arms positioned along the sides of the vehicle spray-paint the metal inside and out, opening and closing doors automatically as the car moves along. They then apply a clear coat to protect the painted surface and give the car a bright shine.

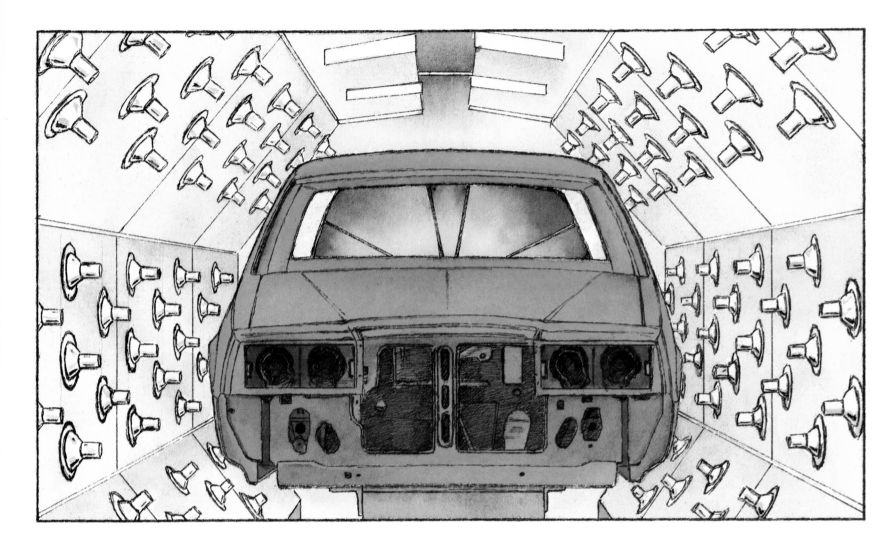

The car now moves into the *drying booth*. Blowers line the walls of the booth and blow out hot air which dries the paint. Once dry, the car is ready for the trim department.

Every car has both hard and soft trim. Hard trim includes the windows and windshield, the dashboard and instrument panel, and the steering column. Soft trim includes the carpets, seats, door pads, and ceiling pads.

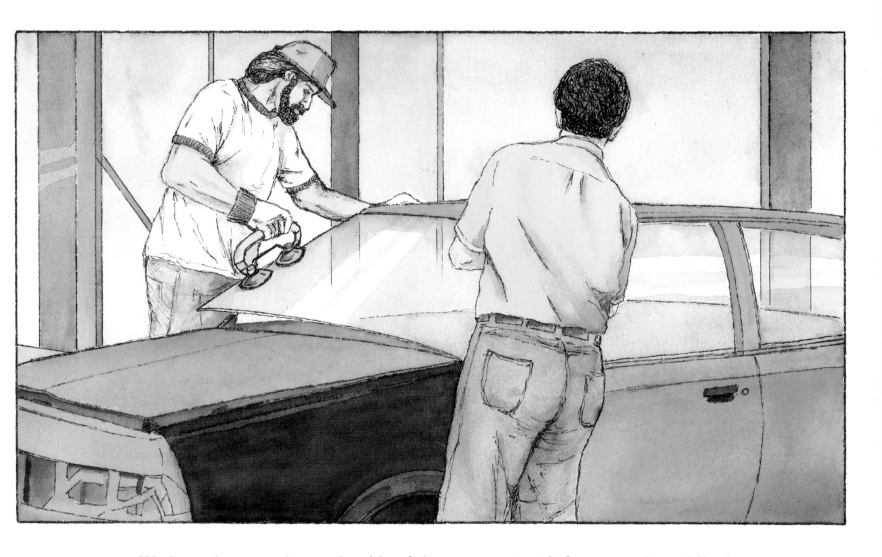

Workers place a pad over the side of the car to protect it from scratches while they finish assembly. To install the windshield, workers apply strong adhesive to the edges of the glass and position it in place with large suction cups. Once the windshield is securely installed, the car moves through a hard water shower to detect any leaks.

Before installing the instrument panel, technicians test it to be sure all parts are working properly. This includes the speedometer, trunk and hood releases, light controls, clock, and other gauges. Then they climb into the car and attach the wires for all the instruments. Finally they move the dashboard into place.

The steering column is now ready to be installed. Workers can quickly and easily install it because it arrives at the plant already assembled. After the remaining hard trim, such as the weather stripping, is installed, the soft trim is ready to be moved into place.

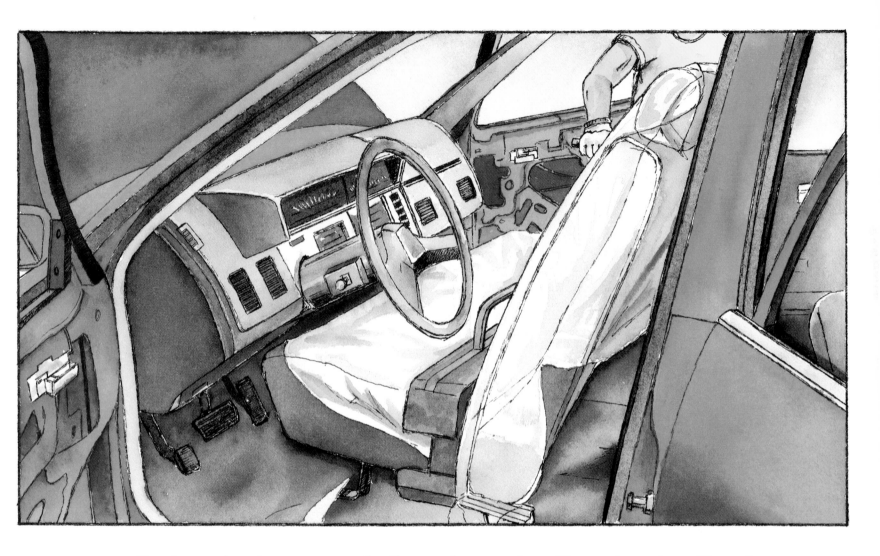

Employees lay the carpets on the floor and secure the ceiling pads to the ceiling of the car. The seats, which skilled upholsterers finish by hand, are moved into place, and the interior of the car is complete. The car now looks like it is ready to go, but there is still nothing under the hood.

The engine is partially assembled when it arrives at the plant, but it must be *dressed* by attaching parts—like the hoses and the *transmission*—before it can be installed.

As the engine moves along this *mini-assembly line* and is dressed, the body of the car moves along on a separate *conveyor belt*. When the two meet, the engine is raised and fitted into the front end of the car. A worker then moves in to secure the engine in place with a special computerized wrench.

Only a few steps remain before the car is complete. The *suspension system*, which is made up of *springs* and *shock absorbers,* is raised up into the car from below. A properly adjusted suspension system helps to provide a smooth and comfortable ride for the passengers in the car.

While the engine and suspension system are being fitted to the body, tires and wheels are being matched on another mini-assembly line. With tires in place, the wheels move down through chutes and roll out to be put in place. Workers stationed around the car mount the wheels.

Standing on its four new wheels, the car moves onto a floor level belt which takes it to the end of the assembly line.

Workers install the bumpers, lights, grillwork, and other finishing touches as the car nears the end of the line. Special details, such as *striping*, are also applied at this point.

To apply striping, a worker mounts a special rack onto each side of the car and then runs a tube of striping paint along this rack to create a smooth, even stripe.

Trained quality inspectors examine the car one last time, although it has passed checkpoints all along the assembly line. Workers have a list of items which they check off as each is examined. Sometimes a minor adjustment may be needed, or sometimes a car must be pulled off the assembly line for further work.

Cars that have passed the final inspection are ready to roll off the line for shipment to car dealers across the country. There they face the toughest inspector of all, the customer.

GLOSSARY

anti-corrosion bath: (**anti** = against; **corrode** = to eat or gnaw away) A bath for an unpainted car which protects the metal against rust.

assembly plant: (**assemble** = to put together; **plant** = factory) The building where cars are put together.

blanking press: A huge machine that cuts shapes out of metal sheets, much like a cookie cutter cuts shapes out of dough.

body shop: A place in the assembly plant where all the parts of the car body and frame are fused together.

computer-aided design (CAD): The process by which people draw objects onto computer screens. The computer allows people to change parts of their design without starting all over again.

conveyor belt: A belt or chain on which objects are moved along a path from one place to another.

dress: The process of attaching to a car engine the parts that make it run, such as hoses, belts and transmission.

drying booth: An area in the assembly plant where freshly painted cars are blown dry.

fuse: To make two pieces of material, like metal or plastic, stick to one another.

gray primer: The first layer applied to unpainted metal.

mass production: (**mass** = many; **produce** = to make) The making of large numbers of a product in a short time period through the use of identical parts and assembly methods.

mini-assembly line: (**mini** = small; **assemble** = to put together) A smaller assembly area within the plant where parts are made ready for the car.

paint booth: A dust–free area where the assembled car body is painted.

prototype: (**proto** = first; **type** = kind) A handmade, working copy of the car to be manufactured. Prototypes are built for testing the design of the car so that any problems can be corrected before production.

sealant: A substance applied to the seams of the car where different pieces are joined together. Sealant prevents water and air from leaking into these cracks.

shock absorbers: Pieces attached underneath the car to let the car bounce gently when it goes over bumps.

side frames: In the sides of the car, side frames act as a support and connector, like a skeleton, for the parts that are attached to the sides of the car.

springs: Strips or wires of steel coiled in a spiral that spring back into shape after being stretched or pressed by the movement of the car.

stamping machine: A large machine that molds doors, hoods, trunks, and body parts from the panels cut in the blanking press.

striping: The detail stripes which are painted onto the car.

suspension system: The springs, shock absorbers, and connecting pieces which work together to keep the car riding smoothly when roads are rough.

transmission: A series of gears which controls the engine's power in a way that allows the car to move at different speeds.

underbody: The bottom or underneath of a car.

wind tunnel: An area in which extremely high winds (of up to 150 miles per hour) are generated to see how it moves around the car. The easier the wind moves around the car, the more efficient the car will be.